G000146779

CHILTERN LANDSCAPES

A collection of photographs portraying the gentle landscape of the Chiltern Hills in South-East England.

BY DOUG KENNEDY

OTHER FORMATS

Chiltern Landscapes is available in two formats, A4: 297mm x 210mm and a pocket size: 160mm x 113mm. Large prints and greetings cards can also be made to order.
Email: sales@doug-kennedy.com

First published by Doug Kennedy Books 2012
Vulcan House, Holly Tree Lane, Cuddington
Buckinghamshire HP18 0BA

Website: www.doug-kennedy.com
© Doug Kennedy 2012
Email: sales@doug-kennedy.com

ISBN 978-0-9574155-1-5

LOCATION OF THE IMAGES

Map of the Chiltern region showing the locations of images in this book. Each number
corresponds to the table on page 40, which shows the grid references and place names.

CHILTERN LANDSCAPES AN INTRODUCTION

The photographs in this book were taken whilst roaming the Chiltern Hills, west of London, in search of it's natural wonders. They are being published in the hope that you will share and enjoy some of the beauty and atmosphere of these gentle hills.

The book traces the seasons, starting in the springtime when beech woods are carpeted in bluebells and the grey tree trunks, like cathedral pillars, tower up to a translucent canopy of newly emerged leaves. It is a joy to stroll the flower-scented footpaths, where sunlight plays through the forest levels in bursts of vibrant green and lights up the purple forest floor. Meadows are alive with new grass and crops are still young enough for the flinty grey soil to show, while hares, rabbits, squirrels and deer can be glimpsed if you walk quietly and enjoy the birdsong.

With the summer, beech leaves darken and the deep forest light shade is broken by brilliant shafts of sunlight illuminating the leafy forest floor. As the damp, muddy footpaths dry out, red campions and foxgloves replace the spring flowers whilst outside the forest, the steep grasslands become carpeted in rock roses, buttercups, poppies and orchids. Here butterflies dance among the flowers; common and chalkhill blues, marbled whites, ringlets and gatekeepers. As crops ripen, the patchwork of fields is now predominantly green, and cottage gardens are full of roses.

With the harvest, the fields are bare once more, strewn with stubble and the hard, knobbly flints that are traditionally used to decorate Chiltern houses. The forests begin to turn yellow and brown, and on a sunny autumn day just before leaf fall, you may find yourself walking through a golden palace where the sunshine shimmers in the misty air. Among the chestnut coloured leaf litter are often strewn mushrooms and toadstools of all shapes, colours and sizes.

In wintertime, the trees are stark and bare, but more light opens up the forests in a peaceful collage of grey and brown. The fields are empty of livestock, or furrowed where the plough has passed, waiting for the year to turn. Being a few hundred feet in altitude, so it often snows, transforming the woods and lanes into snowy wonderlands of frost and snow-rimed trees and Christmas-card cottages. And we dream of the coming of spring.

This is a very managed landscape, where development, farming and nature mingle and often compete. As an Area of Outstanding Natural Beauty, and containing many nature reserves, backed by active residents who love these hills, the landscape and ecology have a good degree of protection. However the ecology of heaths and ancient woods is fragile, and threats are constant. The latest of these is to build the UK's second high speed rail line through the Missenden Valley (see pages 22-25), and there are suggestions that the Green Belt laws are holding up economic development. This book celebrates the beauty of the Chiltern landscape today, and if you want to help to protect it for tomorrow, contact the Chiltern Society (www.chilternsociety.org.uk).

EARLY SPRING

②

Left:

SPRING

THE RIDE UP TO THE OBELISK IN
TRING PARK

This was erected by the Rothschilds and is
known locally as Nell Gwynn's Monument.

③

Opposite:

THE 18TH CENTURY CHURCH OF
ST LAWRENCE, WEST WYCOMBE

With its golden ball, sits high above the village
of West Wycombe on a site that had been in
iron-age hill fort. The church was remodelled
by Sir Francis Dashwood in the eighteenth
century and is remarkable both because the ball
can seat up to eight people and also because he
added the hexagonal flint and stone Dashwood
Mausoleum. He also had the infamous Hell-Fire
Caves excavated under the hill below it, which
ramble deep underground and are decorated
with scenes from the notorious Hellfire Club
(members of which included Shelley and Lord
Byron), which used to meet there. The site, and
the picturesque village of West Wycombe, are
now owned by the National Trust who bought
it from the Dashwood family in the 1930s.

OVERLEAF

The annual carpeting of the forest floor by
bluebells (Hyacinthoides non-scripta) is
possibly the most famous glory of the Chilterns.
The flowers appear in the latter half of April,
and by May great swathes of forest turn into
a brilliant purple carpet, contrasting with the
pale green beech canopy above. As is often the
case with natural phenomena of great beauty,
bluebells are fragile, depending upon soil
that is undisturbed for decades, and not being
trampled upon. Thousands of people make the
journey to experience this blossoming each
year; an experience that depends upon ancient
woods being left undisturbed.

④

Left:

SPRINGTIME IN BEECH FOREST
NEAR SATWELL

With bluebells carpeting the forest floor
and a shining leafy ceiling.

⑤

Right:

SWATHES OF BLUEBELLS NEAR
CHRISTMAS COMMON

LATE APRIL INTO MAY

⑤

Left:

A SOLITARY WALKER ON A PATH
THROUGH BEECH WOODS NEAR
CHRISTMAS COMMON

There are bluebell woods throughout the
Chilterns, and one of the most extensive of
these extends south from this hamlet. If you
continue walking on this path, you pass Stonor
House and eventually arrive at Henley-on-
Thames.

⑥

Below:

A CLOSE-UP OF THE TURF AT SHIRBURN

Showing some of the diversity of flowers,
including rockroses (Helianthemum
nummularium) and bird's-foot trefoil (Lotus
corniculatus). The mix of species is so rich that
as the year progresses, different species will
flower here, and mushrooms will spring up
among them.

⑥

Opposite:

ROCKROSES IN BLOOM ON
SHIRBURN HILL

This part of the western scarp of the Chilterns,
along with the Aston Rowant National Nature
Reserve, have never been ploughed and the
result is an incredibly rich and diverse range of
wildflowers, including several kinds of orchids
blooming in great profusion.

(29)

Left:

A RED KITE

These beautiful birds have become common in the Chilterns since they were re-introduced in the nineties. They had been persecuted to extinction because people thought that they killed livestock, but in fact they are scavengers, feeding mostly on animal corpses, of which there is no shortage owing to the number of road kills as cars get faster and roads get busier.

(29)

Lower left:

ROE DEER RUNNING ACROSS A CHALKY FIELD

If you walk quietly, you will often spy roe deer in groups like this, though most commonly they are found in the woods.

(6)

Opposite:

THE WESTERN SCARP OF THE CHILTERNS

The scarp descends steeply to the ancient Ridgeway route, which is now a long distance footpath, and on to the fertile plain where the river Thame winds to meet Mother Thames at the old settlement of Dorchester-on-Thames. The town of Watlington can be seen below, surrounded by productive farm land. The little airplane flies above the Didcot Power Station in the distance.

Left:

TURVILLE VILLAGE FROM COBSTONE
WINDMILL

Upper right:

TURVILLE COTTAGES, LOOKING TOWARDS
THE WINDMILL

Turville has to be one of the most picturesque villages In England, its brick cottages sitting smugly beneath the white windmill, two hundred feet above. Its ancient name was Thyrefeld, and the 'ville' only appeared in the sixteenth century, at a time when St Alban's Abbey disposed of its ownership of the area. Rather more recently, the little church of St Mary's was used in the television comedy, The Vicar of Dibley, starring Dawn French. The hills and valley are criss-crossed with footpaths, and the lanes are quiet so the Bull and Butcher pub is something of a mecca for walkers, as well as locals seeking a good meal and a pint of Breakspeare's bitter.

Lower right:

ST BARTHOLOMEW CHURCH, FINGEST

Just a mile down the road towards Hambledon and the River Thames lies the small village of Fingest, which contains a fine pub and the twelfth century church of St Bartholomew with its unusual tower.

OVERLEAF

Left:

THE THAMES AT MILL END, NEAR HENLEY

The south side of the Chilterns is bordered by the River Thames between Maidenhead and Goring-on-Thames, winding through its beautiful valley past a historic countryside sprinkled with pretty towns and villages.

Right:

POPPIES AT THE HEAD OF THE
HAMBLEDEN VALLEY

The Hambledon Valley traces a brook from Turville and Fingest, through Skirmett and Hambleden villages to Mill End on the Thames. The valley is a rural idyll with livestock peacefully grazing the meadows and wooded slopes on either side.

6

Left:

MISTY AFTERNOON AT SHIRBIRN

The little bumps are ant hills made by yellow heath ants. In building these, they assist in the spread of plant seeds, which helps explain the great diversity of flowers here.

30

Right:

TEMPLE ISLAND NEAR HENLEY

This is a favoured spot for weddings and other parties, and marks the limit of rowing races from Henley.

OVERLEAF

HENLEY-ON-THAMES

This beautiful, lively town is very favoured, lying on the north bank of the River Thames at one of the most scenic stretches, and the the foot of some of the loveliest parts of the Chilterns. It is a busy market town hosting a college and many businesses whilst remaining a very popular spot with tourists.

31

Left:

VIEW FROM HENLEY BRIDGE OVER
THE ANGEL ON THE BRIDGE PUB

Henley Bridge joins the town to the village of Remenham where the famous Henley Royal Regatta is held. This lasts for four days in late July and, as well as attracting some of the best rowing teams in the world for top level competition, it has become a huge social occasion in the English summer season. The Regatta culminates with a fireworks finale to send the town partying into the Henley Festival a week later.

This image was taken right opposite the Leander Rowing Club clubhouse, who's members including Steve Redgrave have won many Olympic medals. The Angel is a picturesque pub that is a great place to sit and watch the boats and birds on the river whilst enjoying a drink.

31

Right:

LOOKING UP HART STREET FROM
THE RIVER

HIGH SUMMER

Left:
ASTON ROWANT NATIONAL
NATURE RESERVE

Looking west over wildflower meadows in Aston Rowant National Nature Reserve, into Oxfordshire.

Below:
CHALKHILL BLUE BUTTERFLIES

Because the meadows in Aston Rowant are so rich in wildflowers, you can find a plethora of insects, including butterflies. Here are two chalkhill blues feeding on carline thistle

Upper right:
BEECH FOREST IN SUMMER WITHIN WARBURG NATURE RESERVE

Lower right:
GRIM'S DITCH

This is a pre-historic earthwork that meanders through parts of the Chilterns, with extensions in Berkshire, Hampshire and Middlesex. It's use is probably more boundary marking than defensive, and 'Grim' is not a person, but possibly a Norse word for a god.

THE MISSENDEN VALLEY

This lovely valley, running north-west to Wendover, is a transport corridor, for a main road and Chiltern Railway's line to Aylesbury. However, it remains a landscape of great beauty and includes the picturesque towns of Great Missenden and Old Amersham. Sadly, it is currently threatened with a new high speed railway joining London and Birmingham, which will both scar the countryside and be very noisy.

Left:
VIEW OVER FIELDS TOWARDS LITTLE MISSENDEN

Below:
GREAT MISSENDEN

Right:
LITTLE MISSENDEN

Below right:
OLD PETROL STATION IN GREAT MISSENDEN

OVERLEAF

Left:
VIEW OVER PRINCES RISBOROUGH FROM WHITELEAF

Right:
OLD AMERSHAM FROM THE CHURCH TOWER

Ivinghoe Beacon is a spur of the Chilterns, near to their northern extremity. The top is bare, and offers great views in all directions, with the farmland of Buckinghamshire and Bedfordshire some two hundred metres below stretching far into the distance. It is well frequented by walkers, being the start of the Ridgeway and Icknield Way long-distance paths. A further reason for it's popularity is that it is windy, so great for flying kites and model airplanes.

Far left:
COMMON SPOTTED ORCHID
(DACTYLORHIZA FUCHSII)

The top of the Ivinghoe Ridge is chalk grassland, and full of wild flowers. Among the most beautiful of these are orchids, such as the common spotted orchid, pictured here.

Left:
CLUSTERED BELL FLOWER
(CAMPANULA GLOMERATA)

Campanulas, such as harebells, and clustered bell flowers with their intense blue/purple spike of flowers always inspire a sense of wonder at the way something so lovely can just appear in a stretch of grassy heath.

Right:
IVINGHOE BEACON

The chalky pathway to the Ivinghoe Beacon trig point, and the beginning (or end) of the Ridgeway.

FLINT BUILDINGS

Flint is very hard and durable and occurs in nodules in chalk. The nodules are too irregular and small to be used structurally, but set into mortar, flint is extremely durable and looks very attractive, so is a traditional building material in the Chilterns.

Left:
ST MARY MAGDALEN CHURCH, GREAT HAMPDEN

This flint-covered church lies next to Hampden House, at the end of a dead-end road and about a mile from the village. This must have been more for the convenience of the Hobart-Hampden family who built the original manor than for the villagers! This view is from the sunny meadow on the south side of the church.

Above:
HAMBLEDON VILLAGE

Set in the midst of its beautiful valley, is another Chiltern jewel. It is completely unspoiled and its buildings are mostly dressed in flint, giving it a unique character.

Right:
HAMBLEDEN VILLAGE FROM ACROSS THE CRICKET PITCH

AUTUMN

 (29)
Left:
A DEATH CAP TOADSTOOL
(AMANITA PHALLOIDES)
These are quite common in this wood and very poisonous! However you can also find delicious edible mushrooms such as the horn of plenty, and the wood blewitt.

(29)
Lower Left:
THE MAGPIE INKCAP
(COPRINUS PICACEUS)
This mushroom is unusual in that, as it matures, the cap turns into black liquid that is full of spores, and it sort of melts away.

 (22)
Right:
AUTUMN ARRIVES IN NINN WOODS
As the days shorten in October, the dark green beech foliage turns to yellow before it falls in November and adds to the soft, springy depth of leaf litter. This is an ancient wood, which means that it has been forest since at least 1600. Ancient woods are scarce and precious habitats in England: precious for the diverse life forms they contain and also for the well-being of humanity. We put our happiness, and even our existence at peril when we destroy them for the sake of economic development, or of simply getting about even faster.

A wood is not just a wood: because the soil has never been ploughed or fertilised, it is a rich and complex structure that supports this entire ecosystem. One result is that the forest floor is full of fungal fibres from which dozens of species of mushrooms and toadstools spring up each autumn. The trees and fungi are closely connected, and rely upon each other in a symbiotic relationship which means that the trees' ability to thrive depends upon the fungi, and vice-versa.

Britain is very fortunate to have The Woodland Trust, which is a charity that buys woods, particularly ancient woods, and is dedicated to restoring them where necessary and protecting them from development whilst encouraging public access. It also takes on areas to be forested and plants native woodlands that have the potential to develop into areas of great biodiversity. To become a member, go to www.woodland-trust.org.uk.

 17
Far left:
WHITELEAF WOODS, LATE OCTOBER

 23
Left and right:
LONGHILL WOOD NEAR TURVILLE
PARK IN NOVEMBER

OVERLEAF

 17
Left:
WHITELEAF WOODS IN A MOMENT
OF PURE GOLD

 24
Right:
NEEDLE-COVERED ROAD THROUGH
A LARCH WOOD NEAR NETTLEBED
Sadly, this wood was felled the following
year owing to a fungal disease that had been
imported along with garden centre plants.

WINTER

Left:
THE COOMBE HILL MONUMENT,
NEAR BUTLER'S CROSS

If you have the energy to make the steep climb up from the village below, you are said to be able to see five counties from this hill. We are in Buckinghamshire, overlooking Aylesbury Vale, and can certainly see Oxfordshire to the south. But however many other counties you actually can see, the view is magnificent, so it's a popular hike to the top and along the ridge even on a cold winters day like this.

Right:
CHILTERN SCARP

The view south along the Chiltern scarp from the monument on a frosty November afternoon.

OVERLEAF

Left:
ICE AND SNOW-COVERED FIELD,
HAMPDEN

Right:
SNOW CREATES A WINTER WONDERLAND
ON A LANE NEAR CHEQUERS

Above:
SIGN POST ON WAIN HILL

CAMERA NOTES

Most of the photographs in this book were taken with a Panasonic DMC-G1 camera, apart from a few that were taken before 2009 which tend to have lower resolution but are included for the sake of the subject. The Panasonic G1 is light and small enough to carry in a pouch around my waste whilst I am walking or running but has a range of lenses, of which I used two giving me a range of 14-200mm. The camera resolution is 10 Megapixels with software that makes it very fast and flexible. A digital SLR camera would have been larger and weigh several times as much without a significant quality improvement.

40